To THE GIRL
IN THE MIRROR -

She needs you ♡

xoxo -

AMY LOGAN

Full Heart Publishing

ISBN-13: 978-0-9890465-5-8
Title font courtesy of Denise Bentulan

DEDICATION

To all of you beautiful people reading this right now,
who maybe just don't see it yet, here's the truth:
you were born because the world knew *you* would make a
difference. And you won't always know when that *exact*
moment will happen, but I promise you, it will.

And because of that,
this book is dedicated to you, your perseverance, your
strength, your kindness, and your ability to keep going,
no matter how tired you may become.
This world needs you.
True Story.

ACKNOWLEDGMENTS

Thank you to my family – *all of you* – who have always
cheered me on, even when I didn't feel like playing anymore.
And thank you to everyone who has crossed my path, stayed
on my path, or left my path. Because of you, my path became
better, kinder, tougher, stronger.
I wouldn't be here without any of you.
And I can't thank you enough.

xoxo,
amy

THE GIRL IN THE MIRROR

Author's Note:

There is a journal at the end of this book, but please, journal along the way if you like. The pages are left with a lot of open space on purpose. Doodle, create, write down your thoughts as they come to you. This book is my *personal* story, but truth be told, I wrote it for you. Here we go.

"There once was a time when I liked myself.

I can't really remember

when that all changed,

or why it all did,

or who is to blame,

but that doesn't matter because

right here, right now,

my reflection - it shows me the changes

and how

I'd rather be looking at somebody else...

and not looking,

and staring...

and hating myself... ."

A long time ago, *that's* who I was.

I was like so many others

who suddenly discover

that differences matter

and instead of being me…

I would so much rather be

the girl with the blonde hair

over there

or the

one thin and tall.

Or sometimes?

Sometimes, I'd rather not be here at all.

It's true.

And it makes me sad

that once upon a time I thought I had it so bad,

and had I followed through

and changed who I was

and where I came from,

I would've missed out and never have seen

the me…

I've become.

The me I was born and intended to be…

the one in the mirror looking back at me.

Right here.

Right now.

You know you can't always see it

and you can't always be it

at the age of 13,

or 16,

or sometimes passed 22.

We stare and compare…

and would rather be you.

So we hide and suppress all

the sadness inside.

And we feel as if our whole insides

have died.

But they haven't.

Please hear what I say -

you *have* to fight through to see another day.

I can't make this up.

It hurts, and it's real.

I know...

you can't change your mind

when you can't change how you feel.

But darling…

You need to hold on.

You have it inside you to love and be strong.

See, I know this.

I know this so all too well

that your life right now may *seem* like a hell

but it's normal.

You're not crazy and you're not alone.

And had *I* given in so many years ago

I'd never have seen the life I now know.

And now?

The way I can influence those and how

I matter,

when never I thought,

and into the media

I bought…

and I bought.

You know,

the world sets you up

with all of these things,

and all these perfections

it tells you to bring.

But what they *don't* tell you?

Is

    there's

        no

            such

                thing.

And although they insist

         and insist

            and insist,

the perfections *you* seek from the

        truth that *they* twist?

        You'll never stop seeking…

because

they don't exist.

It's true.

See, the reason *you're* here,

the reason *you* came

is that you're unique and

you're *not* the same as everyone else.

Thank God that's the truth!

And I'm here to tell you – I'm living proof

that in time, *give it time*

because right now you *don't* see it

but that doesn't mean that you *won't* see it.

Give it time.

Sweet darling?

Just hang on.

Don't give up on yourself or the day.

There are so many *amazing* things coming your way.

And if you *hold on*

and *stop hating* who you see,

you may end up *loving*

who you were meant to be…

the girl in the mirror.

Just smile at her

and know that in time

you'll look back at her

and thank her for all of

the strength that she gave you

through the years that have passed,

and your life...

... that she saved you.

You *are* worth saving, girl in the mirror.

Your life – you can't see it yet very clear

but it's coming and it *needs* you

so don't be afraid

of yourself anymore

or the choices you've made.

You are worth *every* second of *every* day

that you've lived so far,

and with more on the way.

So, girl in the mirror?

Go easy.

Be gentle and kind to yourself.

You *weren't* created to be someone else.

It was you - *YOUR SOUL* - the universe birthed.

If that doesn't convince you

you came here with worth

then hear what *I* say, since I've been there too:

"You matter, sweet darling, because *YOU* ...

were born *you.*"

Everything else, our bodies our "shell"?

That's not who we are so don't buy what they sell.

You're frightened, and the world

it plays on that fear.

So right now, just hang tight,

sweet girl in the mirror...

because your purpose awaits you.

The path your life's paving -

it's carefully creating a life that's worth saving.

And even though some days

just seem like survival...

your future self?

She's expecting your arrival.

And she's absolutely amazing.

XOXO

A Note From Amy:

My dear friend reading this right now,

*I want you to know that I get you. I. Get. You.
Like some of you, for years, I struggled with depression, an
eating disorder, feeling less than, feeling like I had no real value
or purpose. The screams in my head knocking me down were* **so
loud** *over the years that it muffled and distorted anything good
anyone ever had to say to me. I get you.*

And this is where you need to trust me.

*It wasn't until I turned forty(Wow! That's a big number.) that I
realized my true purpose, that I saw my value, that I saw the
reason the world kept me here. (Don't freak out if you are in
your teens or early twenties. You may find yours sooner than
that. But for me? Forty.) The point is, that you* **will** *find it.
The point is that you* **have** *to hang on and never* **ever** *give up
on yourself. The point is that you* **have** *to start treating yourself
as the future girl in the mirror. She needs you. And you need
her. And wherever you are in your life right now, whatever you
feel is more powerful than you, I'm telling you there is* **nothing**
*more powerful than our thoughts and how we speak to ourselves.
So, every time that awful voice starts kicking you in the head?
Pick up this book and read it. Then read it again. Then look at
yourself in the mirror and say, "I've got this. The world needs
me. I'm pretty fricken awesome!" and then go about your day.
Stop knocking yourself down all the time. The world probably
does a pretty good job of that already, right? Why join 'em?
Future you wouldn't put up with that. So present you shouldn't
either. You've got an amazing future ahead of you… and you,
sweet darling, are ready for it.*

xoxo, amy

****

So – this is for you. Writing down my thoughts always helped me to get out of my own head and focus on other things - which was not and is not always easy to do. But, this helps.

*Don't **EVER** forget how **amazing** and **important** and **needed** you are. Even if you don't see it or feel it right now, there's someone in your future **on your path** who is **expecting** you and **needing** you to show up. Here's to moving forward and showing up. Grab your pen.* ☺

****

Thoughts * Hopes * Dreams * Wishes

_____

_____

_____

_____

_____

_____

_____

_____

_____

_____

_____

_____

_____

AMY LOGAN

List of Positive Words:

What, if anything, bothers me at the moment?

What do I love, right now, about myself?

_____
_____
_____
_____
_____
_____
_____
_____
_____
_____
_____
_____
_____
_____
_____
_____
_____
_____
_____
_____
_____
_____
_____
_____
_____
_____
_____
_____

What can I change, do I *want* to change,
and make more positive?

_____

_____

_____

_____

_____

_____

_____

_____

_____

_____

_____

_____

_____

_____

_____

_____

_____

_____

_____

_____

_____

_____

_____

_____

_____

_____

How can I plan to make those changes right here, right now?

Where would I like to see myself five years from now?
Ten years from now?

If I could have anything in the world, here's what I want:

_____
_____
_____
_____
_____
_____
_____
_____
_____
_____
_____
_____
_____
_____
_____
_____
_____
_____
_____
_____
_____
_____
_____
_____
_____
_____
_____

AMY LOGAN

A few other things…

A reminder of the things I *love*, and why:

People, Bands, Songs, Foods, Restaurants, Colors, Outfits

AMY LOGAN

Other thoughts:

_____

_____

_____

_____

_____

_____

_____

_____

_____

_____

_____

_____

_____

_____

_____

_____

_____

_____

_____

_____

_____

_____

_____

_____

AMY LOGAN

****

Here's an extra thought for you…

*"Because you **are** worth the fight."*

Always.

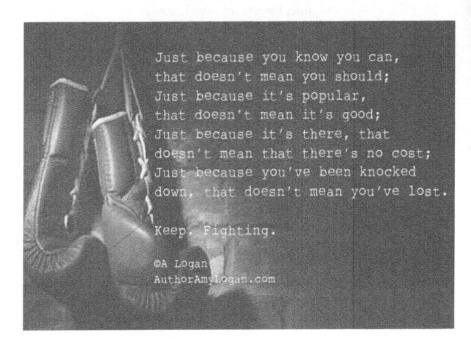

Just because you know you can,
that doesn't mean you should;
Just because it's popular,
that doesn't mean it's good;
Just because it's there, that
doesn't mean that there's no cost;
Just because you've been knocked
down, that doesn't mean you've lost.

Keep. Fighting.

©A Logan
AuthorAmyLogan.com

****

RESOURCES

National Suicide Prevention Lifeline
  1-800-273-8255
  crisistextline.org
  suicidepreventionlifeline.org

National Association of Anorexia Nervosa and
Associated Disorders
  Helpline: 630-577-1330
  anad.org

The National Institute of Mental Health
  1-866-615-6464
  nimh.nih.gov

National Eating Disorder Association.
  1-800-931-2237
  nationaleatingdisorders.org

The Body is Not An Apology
  1-202-681-3052
  thebodyisnotanapology.com

Be Nourished
  1-503-288-4104
  benourished.org

ABOUT THE AUTHOR

Amy Logan is the author of four inspirational children's books: *A Girl With A Cape* (2013), *A Girl With A Cape and Her Jar of Pennies* (2014), and *A Girl With A PINK Cape* (2015), and *A Boy With A Cape* (2016). She is also the founder of the *Kindness Gala,* which is a red-carpet celebration and fundraising event for local charities (KindnessGala.com).

Amy holds a Bachelor's Degree in Speech Pathology, a Masters Degree in Teaching, and 10 years Leadership Experience in the Direct Sales Industry. Through her work and life experience, Amy teaches that right now, right where you are, is exactly where you are supposed to be on your journey so far, whether you realize it or not. She insists that we were all born with the incredible ability to have a huge impact on our world; that we were all born because the world *knew* we would make a difference. She resides in Illinois with her husband, two kids, and two dogs. Who are obnoxious. The dogs, not the kids. Although some days it's the kids. Or the husband. Or all of the above.

For more information on her books, her Empowerment Talks, or what she's currently working on, visit her websites: AuthorAmyLogan.com or GotYourCape.com.

Made in the USA
Monee, IL
02 February 2020

21156384R10049